This book is a precious gift to my Beautifu'

Creative Granddaughter!

Eliza

Happiest Birthday Ever!

With Prayers from my heart, songs from my

soul, and all my Love & Hugs!

From Grandma Irene

With Special Blessings to ALL the Children of

the world. (Both young & old 😉)

♥Always Remember YOU are LOVED!♥

First Edition: Eliza Grandma Loves You!

Publisher: The Lopez Cottage Publishing

Author: Grandma Irene Lopez

Cover and book designed & hand sketched by:

Grandma Irene Lopez

Cataloging in publication data has been applied for and is available from the Library of Congress.

ISBN#978-1-7348348-3-3

Copyright 2022

<u>Bible verses from:</u> The Holy Bible New King James Version-Thomas Nelson, Inc. & Holy Bible New Living Translation Giant Print NLT Personal Size Tyndale House Publishers Carol Stream Illinois.

Eliza,
Always remember to begin your day by giving gratitude to God.

"Praise the Lord!

Oh! give thanks to the Lord, for

He is good!

For His mercy endures forever."

Psalm chapter 106 Verse 1

Eliza,
Always make your
bed.

It's a good habit
and will start your
day in a positive
way!

Eliza,
Brush your teeth
and smile at that
Beautiful Girl in the
mirror.
As you look in the
mirror can you see
how perfectly YOU!
God made YOU!

Eliza,
It's dress up time.
Put on your favorite
dress and shoes.
Sprinkle perfume and
brush your hair.
Dress with
confidence and wear
your wisdom well. But
do not forget to sparkle
and shine with your
beautiful smile!

Eliza,
Sit at the table for a healthy breakfast.

Always tell your Mom and Dad THANK YOU!

"Honor your father and your mother, that your days may be long upon the land which the Lord your God is giving you."

Exodus chapter 20 verse 12

Eliza,
Gather your
backpack, lunch, and
sweater; it's time to
go to school.

Psalm chapter 121 verse 7

Eliza,
Always surround yourself with beautiful souls. They will be your friends and share fun times with you.

"**Walk with the wise** and become wise; associate with fools and get in trouble."

Proverbs chapter 13 verse 20

Eliza,
When you are in
class, remember the
power of asking. Raise
your hand with courage
and be brave.

"Ask, and it will be given to
you, Seek, and you will find;
knock, and it will be opened to
you."

Matthew chapter 7 verse 7

Eliza,

Always respect your teachers, have fun with your classmates, and appreciate your faculty. Above all, spread kindness everywhere you go and with everyone you meet.

"She opens her mouth with wisdom, and the teaching of kindness is on her tongue."

Proverbs chapter 31 Verse 26

Eliza,

Always thank God

for your lunch and
enjoy it with your
friends at school.

**"Give us today
Our Daily Bread"**

Matthew chapter 6 verse 11

Eliza,
If you see a friend who needs a bit of encouragement.
Be brave and compassionate to cheer them up!

"So, encourage each other and build each other up, just as you are already doing."

1st Thessalonians chapter 5 verse 11

Eliza,

picking you up now
and the day at school is
over.

Great Job! It's
family time to share
your day!

Eliza,
Family are the
people God chose to be
with you to teach you
everything they know
about life. God chose
them to take care of
you and to love you.

"I will praise You, for I am
fearfully and wonderfully made;
Marvelous are Your works, and
that my soul knows very well."
Psalm chapter 139 verse 14

Eliza,
Its time for **rest** and **relaxation** before you do your chores and homework. You had a long day at school. Its ok to shut your eyes and take a nap. Your chores can be done when you awake. You may do your homework after dinner. But for now, rest.

"He makes me lie down in green pastures; He leads me beside the still water." Psalm chapter 23 Verse 2

Eliza,

Look at the Chalkboard and review your chores for the day.

- ⭐ Vacuum
- ⭐ Clean your room
- ⭐ Rake the leaves

"Direct your children onto the right path, and when they are older, they will not leave it."

Proverbs chapter 22 verse 6

Eliza,
It's dinner time!
Can you smell
what's cooking? It's
time to sit at the table
with the entire family;
and share conversation
with sunshine's &
sprinkles (showers).

<u>Sunshines</u> = are positive things that
happened that day.
<u>Sprinkles</u> = are not so great things that
happened that day.

Eliza,
After dinner
ALWAYS help Mom
and Dad with the
clean-up.
It's fun and makes
for great conversations
with Mom and Dad.

"Quality time with Mom
& Dad, making
memories."

Eliza,
Are you ready to
open your
journal/planner to see
what your homework
assignments are?

Readers are Leaders!
Write your story!
Be a Great Listener!
ALWAYS be learning!

Eliza,

You deserve a nice warm bath.

Relax and enjoy the bubbles and lavender aromas of the soaps.

Eliza,
May the army of
Angels surround you
ALWAYS!
May the good Lord
bless you with a
peaceful sleep.
May your Mom and
Dad be with you when
you awake.
~AMEN ~

Big Love Grandma irene

<u>Grandma irene's words of wisdom</u>

Eliza, please know that your life is
a precious gift from God.

What you create and decide to do
with your life is your gift to God.

Always show love and kindness
and be wise in all your decisions.

<u>Write</u> your <u>Goals and Dreams</u>;
and <u>always have a plan</u>.
(Place them in front of you to view every day)

<u>Appreciate</u> every precious
moment and be in that moment.

<u>**Tell your Mom and Dad how
much you love them**</u>. Let them know
how happy you are that God blessed
you with them!